A Map of Every Undoing

Alicia Elkort

STILL
HOUSE
PRESS

Copyright © 2022 by Alicia Elkort.
FIRST EDITION
All rights reserved.

No part of this book may be reproduced without written permission from the publisher.

All inquiries may be directed to:
  Stillhouse Press
  4400 University Drive, 3E4
  Fairfax, VA 22030
  www.stillhousepress.org

Stillhouse Press is an independent, student- and alumni-run nonprofit press based out of Northern Virginia and established in collaboration with the Fall for the Book festival.

Cover Image: Alexandra Eldridge

Library of Congress Control Number: 2022913655
ISBN-13: 978-1-945233-18-0

ADVANCE PRAISE FOR <u>A MAP OF EVERY UNDOING</u>

A Map of Every Undoing tends its wounds with meticulous prosody—a dazzling display of language and voluminous vulnerability, each poem in Elkort's collection is as much a bounty on the tongue as it is a feast for the collective hurts hungering in all of us. "I am safe in the no-/where" Elkort writes, "this soft chapel," but these poems are never *nowhere*—they embody every *every*, clattering against the reverb of physical, emotional, and spiritual harms. These poems brandish a bladed wit that is at times both for and despite its readers, threading together a tapestry of what is most profoundly human: resilience, resistance, and the slant light of self-love.

    Dr. Diamond Forde, author of *Mother Body*

Elkort's poems surprise us at every turn with their fierce gaze, candid wit, and unflinching intelligence. She distills the bewildering tumult and turbulence that is our existence into song. Her voice, which demands and deserves our attention, is nimble, vivid, and energetic.

    Eric Pankey, author of *Augury* and *Crow-Work*

Akin to Persephone "blazing a sadness" to the underworld, Alicia Elkort's remarkable debut *A Map of Every Undoing* takes the reader on an excoriating odyssey through childhood trauma. Elkort's poems spotlight sexual abuse and survival as she inquires "Can you pour fear into a glass? / Shatter it against the wall?" These poems are that shattering. They are emblems of the speaker's strength as she moves through a merciless world of predators, caught between "the terror & the non-terror." *A Map of Every Undoing* is an address to those who have wronged, as well as to those who have been harmed, while also functioning as a reclamation of a woman's power in the face of deathly erasure: "I write my escape, / blood drying on page after page, / folios of fire poppies." Each of Elkort's lines is so freighted with anguish and a serrated grace that I want to quote her repeatedly. Though these poems move through rot and rage, they are alchemized into a thriving survival that so poignantly, and pointedly, ask, "Who am I to speak of beauty? Who am I not to?"

    Simone Muench, author of *Wolf Centos* and *Orange Crush*

Alicia Elkort's dazzling debut, *A Map of Every Undoing*, offers both lovesong to the strength of women and girls and healing balm for those who've been abused, bullied, unacknowledged, unsung, or unloved. These deft, lyric poems draw from familial and personal history, the worlds of myth, literature, and art, and the speaker's own vast imagination to create a cosmos capable of both honoring and healing the wound at the center, stitching "wings to birds / bird to wings… / making a nest of every cry & terror." Elkort, with her enduring eye to detail, recognizes and names the beauty that surrounds and uplifts the women and girls whose lives have been ravaged by pain, and who still, miraculously, choose love, choose "a hand / on the heart, a reassuring word… / love … a dedication, not a gift" in order to assure that "somewhere the pattern interrupts." This collection is both vast as the "unfathomable universe" and personal as beloveds sharing a quiet home-spun dream ("Here is my hand & here is laughter & here is solace / & here is my house where I live by a tree"). These poems are lithe and robust at once, filled with wisdom, care, and patience of a true healer. I love this collection completely.

    Jenn Givhan, author of *Belly to the Brutal* and *River Woman, River Demon*

If part of healing is a search for form, then Alicia Elkort's collection *A Map of Every Undoing* twines this personal search with its lyrical mirror-partner, laying out new paths of feeling over broken sidewalks of sonnets, prose poems, elegies, and dreams. "O / broken sidewalk / your windows are open," as she says in the first poem. The book moves from unsettling trouble toward a lush and quiet joy, or at least a series of questions about joy. Elkort's poems begin in experience but, through inquiry, move to new places in the mind.

    Ed Skoog, author of *Mister Skylight*, *Rough Day*, and *Run the Red Lights*

With a language unpretentious and unapologetic, the poems of Alicia Elkort's extraordinary *A Map of Every Undoing* unveil a territory of sexual violence ("the man who raped me / wore a yellow shirt"), tenderness ("Imagine you want to feed her / pomegranate seeds"), and daring intimacy ("Now comes the opening of the heart."). The "map" in this book is more than a map of placement that tells us where we are. Alicia Elkort offers a map of search and possibilities; an invitation to explore all the places where we could be, the core of who we are ("The highest form of gratitude […] is feeling / grateful for the worst experience / Compassion is the only antidote. /[…] I am not there, yet."

    Mariano Zaro, author of *Decoding Sparrows*

"Sometimes pain is the call of a wound that needs tending, and sometimes it is the sting of its healing."

Melissa Febos

Contents

In Praise of a Broken Sidewalk   1

One

Wherever You Go / Notes from My New Mexico Journal   5
Sonnet for the Man Who Invaded My Childhood or
Only Alchemy Can Redeem a Life   8
ceiling (n.) (12c.) from Latin celare "to hide"
probably influenced by Latin caelum "heaven, sky"   9
I am fashioned from a gourd   12
The solar plexus chakra is associated   13
This Body Is a Warehouse   14
Grandmother says *If I were twenty, I'd burn my fucking bra*   16
Daisies   17
Bullied Girl   20
You're supposed to be writing a love song to yourself   21
Sometimes I Imagined a Knife   22
The Crone Who Appears in My Dreams,
or When Will We Stop Hurting Ourselves?   24
Medusa   27
A Tale Not Told   30
You Don't Have to Be Good   32
The Sparrow   34
These days are hard   35

Two

A Map of Every Undoing   39
Witness   40

Throwing Stones	41
My Sister is a Mermaid at the Bottom of the Pool	42
Triptych in A Minor	44
Sonnet for Icarus' Older Sister Who Would Have Invented the Aeroplane Had She Not Been Married Off for Gold. Also, She Can Divine the Future.	49
A Walk with Mist at Sunset	50
Cutting Diamonds	51
On driving all night to find the shaman who will help me &	54
The Sweet Balm of Dappled Roses	56
You Must Not Disappear	59
Before We Break	60
Rare As Red Beryl	62
Scheherazade's Reflections on Her Wedding Night	63
It began with a flower in bloom,	64
Red	65
A Girl Needs Her Mother	70
All the Goodness of the World	72

Three

It's dark & the ghost	75
Rose Petals	76
A Nest of Every Cry	79
Inside Every Story	80
The Opening of the Heart	81
Sunday Morning	82
Anahata :: Un-struck	84
I Stay with My Parents' Elder Friends	

Who Live On an Island in France (Île De Ré) &	
at Eighteen I Learn How Music Heals	86
Perseus Turns Seriphus to Stone	
(So He No Longer Feels the Weight of His Burden)	87
I Wish You Were Here	89
The Artist Has a Powerful Hunger,	
or the Artist Feels as Though She Can Fly	91
Sunset in the California Desert	92
After An Exhaustive Study of the Girdle of Venus	95
Hay Truck	96
We've Both Lost Patience for Men with Indigo Hands	97
Grandmothers, what I want to know	99
Galaxies	101
She runs to the edge of time in pink stilettos.	103
Acknowledgments	105
Notes	109

for the long arc of healing, which always bends toward love

In Praise of a Broken Sidewalk

Now I accept your jagged dandelion
flowers, taken root in the detritus & today
we'll worship edges, you too
are only a guest in this world—
the ficus buckles the street it's the disrup-
tion I admire, the ways
a child must navigate the up tilt of rag-
ged concrete or the skateboarder learns
to lift rather than catch in the crackle I haven't
understood the imperfect of this world, the
beauty, O
broken sidewalk
your windows are open, your
doors ajar, let Nature unlade
her yellow globes & us
rejoice, for tomorrow we all turn
to seed.

One

Wherever You Go / Notes from My New Mexico Journal

The first time I had consensual sex was with my friend's boyfriend.

He told me they had broken up for the summer so they could fuck around.

I believed him as he rode me like an angry hyena.

I never said stop.

Still, there's humor.

The diaphragm scooched out of my hands, launched across the room.

Clear jelly splattered across the wall, a Rorschach of betrayals.

I wanted my virginity out of the way, & he read complicated fiction.

Imagine, Susan said, referring to a news article, *your first time, to a predator.*

As if she'd never heard about the guy who sexually assaulted the ten-year-old girl.

Imagine I am a ten-year-old girl.

Virginity should be a construct of consent.

Grandmother remembered me in the back seat of the Dodge Dart saying fantastical.

I was four & she thought that was stupendous.

Forgive me for writing flowery epiphanies.

I like the high notes, where wind in the trees caresses the bruised body.

Where the open sky opens.

Where nature lifts the brutal tattoo of rape, match cut to mountain.

I rescue the dog from the cliff & feel his tongue across my face.

Or get the guy in the end, on his knee, betrothing a kaleidoscope of good.

The world is at least 51% good, 53% on a clear, sunny day.

But this life, this quartered vein, the soft stench of humiliation & shame.

I've been waiting for the white horse & the savior.

I know. I am my own savior.

One pill of ecstasy left me with unadulterated joy.

How to remember joy while drowning in a suicide's ocean?

Deborah says *disassociation* is not *dissociation*.

[dih-soh-see-ey-shuhn] Psychiatry :: the splitting off of a group of mental processes from the main body of consciousness as in amnesia or certain forms of hysteria.

I lifted my self to the ceiling.

Everything goes white, still.

But who has not been turned to salt reaching for a daffodil?

The highest form of gratitude [pulling the sweet & bitter into a tapestried life] is feeling grateful for the worst experience—

Compassion is the only antidote.

Just last week I wanted to yell *Unhand me you rankest compound of villainous smell that ever offended nostril* to at least five people.

I'm not there, yet.

Sonnet for the Man Who Invaded My Childhood or Only Alchemy Can Redeem a Life

after Terrance Hayes

I lock you in a locket, a rose gold & amethyst poem,
hang you from a hook in the tool shed, by the guns—
I don't own guns, but this is my secret invective & here,
my rifle is cocked & loaded. Can you feel the softness
of the sanded myrtle wood? Imagine her tree, the wind
in her leaves? There's redemption in this hellfire barrel
as it stares you down. Your scream is one broken loop &
salvation lands so far up these back roads, most likely
no one will hear you. Can you hear the whippoorwills?
Love is always in the air, but you'll have to wash up
in someone else's tub—mine is filled with blood & baby
teeth. I'm editing words as I go, the threat of you, erased.
The door to the shed sticks crooked, & an iron bar damns
everything inside to melting when the fires come.

ceiling (n.) (12c.) from Latin celare "to hide" probably influenced by Latin caelum "heaven, sky"

What I leave out is
    the endless white
        where I rise

to save myself,

    no bone, cartilage—a distance in fog.
    I shallow my breath

to almost death,
my girl-heart beating
    & not beating, absorbed

into plaster & the dried moisture
of tears, lifting—

    I am a child
        in the arms of a fire-

man,   only, there is no one coming
        to save me.
    I disappear
        & aware-

ness becomes cradled
emptiness, like sky

    only in all senses
        the absence of every shade.

I am safe in the no-
where, this soft chapel,
while below,
the grip,
    the spit,
        the scorched thrust
of a grown man. Bruises

ink my body   down.

        Can you pour fear into a glass?
        Shatter it against the wall?

The scream is the jilt
    of my own voice.

I will kill your brother

I am alabaster,

    a carved cherub
    with wings,
        crumbling. How can I be both

above & below & cool
to the touch?

    I am a cloistered ocean,

no waves or seabird sounds. My fists useless,
        hips pinioned—

the terror & the non-terror.
I fold the whole soft sheet of me

           & then again, a quiet child

I am not here &
there is no one here.

      When I try to &
          cannot remember—

say balm, say still,
        say numb.

I am fashioned from a gourd

carved with an ordinary awl.
I am the bluest mountain
beyond the desert where Moses
wept. I am ribbed flaxen & sweet
peas dusting the air—
nine shooting stars transfixed
against a violent sky.
I am candles burning each Friday night,
stubborn and proud. Esther's granddaughter,
daughter of Edythe, great-granddaughter
of Rosalie and Anna. I am a shot
of whiskey before bed and a bicycle ride
Sunday morning while the city sleeps
beneath alabaster fog. I am one year
in a hospital bed as my father relearns
walking on polio-battled bones, a memory
that will carry him through his years.
I am the party where my parents met,
jazz musicians drumming through the Cold War.
I am a ballerina, a perfect arabesque
like silk, like humming.
I make landfall where New Mexico
and Russia converge on the axis—
sopapillas with honey and braided chiles
hanging in the larder, black tea
with a sugar cube on the tongue.
I am from the hope of immigrants
with nothing to lose but life.

The solar plexus chakra is associated

with the color yellow—
        rows of aspens, tendered corn silk,

yellow jackets in picnic sweet tea,
        street signs, tender buds

of ranunculus, mango, lemon, papaya,
        yellow paint beneath

white paint on the neighbor's fence.
        Someone somewhere else

has yellow curtains. The book says
        wear yellow to encourage

confidence, happiness, stability.
        Yellow spinning,

swirling shrapnel, dizzy yellow
        to the knee, to the ground—

the man who raped me
        wore a yellow shirt.

This Body Is a Warehouse

You enter from the alley.
You turn the switch.
A bulb incandesces the hallway.
There are doors on both sides.
You choose—third door on the right—
and turn the faded yellow knob.
You enter slowly.
The room is dark, the air fetid.
Your eyes acclimate.
Inside is a nine-year-old girl standing by herself.
Her body's dewy light exposes the room.
Her disheveled hair slips across her face.
You recognize her shirt as your shirt.
She looks up.
She lifts her left hand and points.
You look in the direction of her finger.
Your knees buckle.
He is on top of her.
She can't breathe.
The light in the room is gone.
You can feel his arms around her throat.
You can't breathe.
He pushes her into the floor.
You are against the floor,
splinters at your neck.
You look away.
You look back at her.

She is still pointing.
You look again.
He has turned her on her stomach.
Your back hurts.
A scream hammers through your body.
You protect your ears with your hands.
The glass in the windows shatters.
The discordance rises from deep inside this building.
You are running for the door.
Serrated window-glass trips your feet.
You fall, hard.
You get up.
Blood is running down your legs.
You run toward candle flame.
A voice says, *It'll be all right.*
You don't know if it will be all right.
You know you will go back.
You will go back.
Take the girl with you.
Feed her salted marrow.
Comb her hair.

Grandmother says *If I were twenty, I'd burn my fucking bra*

It's the only time I've ever heard her swear. She shows me the indents
on her shoulders from bra straps holding heavy breasts all those years

rubs the depressions like they're tiny animals. She's sitting at her dressing
table. I'm fourteen, wearing her pearls and blue eye shadow, massaging

her neck as we look in the mirror. She laughs for swearing, grabs my hand,
caresses the inside of my palm. *Crazy what we do to be pretty.*

She's trying to protect me. *Burn your bra*—only I don't need one. My breasts
have stopped growing. My periods have stopped. I'm so hungry, I'm carving

holes inside my gut for the ballet girls to admire my skinny thighs, flat stomach.
I'm fourteen, standing behind my grandmother in the mirror, trying to disappear.

Daisies

Duncan left a bouquet of limp daisies
in my locker and the other boys sniffed me
in the hall, rubbed my ass, laughed.
When I summoned the courage to tell
Mr. Paris about the boys and their hands,
he leered, "I bet you like it," exaggerating
the i in like for effect. I didn't liiiiike it
any more than I liked Patti punching me
in the locker room, tripping me in the gym.
When she gave me the silent treatment,
I felt relieved. But she was just another girl
whose father unzipped himself between
episodes of *I Dream of Jeannie*, a girl
who thought beating a classmate
half her size would help her grow
wings. But when she jumped
from the roof of a nine-story walkup,
her wings weren't there. Maybe
that didn't happen. Maybe there was no
father, no blood. Maybe she finished
high school and became a bond trader
on Wall Street. Or maybe I found her
on a porn site with too much lipstick,
cracking a whip. I only know that
when I read her obit on the Internet,
I wondered why I was still scared.

~

At Dawn's slumber party
twelve-year-olds watched *Night of the Living Dead*
projected onto a screen when Dawn's boxer
pinned me to the floor and did the nasty
on my back. I tried disappearing
into the floorboards, but found myself
laughing with the other girls. No one knew
I had already been humped
by a sweaty man with a moustache.
Maybe the dog could smell the degradation
and did what animal instinct dictated—
dominate the dominated.

The next day I hung out my eleventh floor
bedroom window, watching people below.
Did you know each person has a distinct gait?
Like a signature. Like the way shame
etches different lines across each face.
I turned up the Rolling Stones as far
as the dial would go and jumped
around my room in a training bra
and pink tutu, screeching the lyrics
to *Paint It Black* at top pitch.
I sang the song over and over
punching air, throwing pillows,

twirling like a dervish. When my parents
came home, I turned off the music
and did my homework.

~

Duncan put the dead daisies in my locker
because I wouldn't talk to him anymore.
I adored Duncan, his worn copy
of *Catcher in the Rye* peering
from the inside pocket of his navy jacket,
his blue eyes blazing a sadness
I had no capacity to understand.
When he said I love you, I hated him.

Bullied Girl

Bullied girl hides / her scrawny self / pulls a carrot from her bag and chews / they make fun of her body / *too skinny* / they make fun of her size / *too small* / her propensity for learning / *too smart* / her curly hair / too curly / coming from California / *too crazy* / her birth religion / *can we see your tail and btw you killed Jesus* / daddy says don't listen / you are kind girl / silly girl / loves-kittens girl / b u l l i e d girl knows he means well / but words like those don't lengthen her spine / because the long dagger of spite / where the merciless abandon all good for / the un-soft shiny veneer of / hate / a whole class of eyes / lashes with the long shame / she buckles every day / she buckles / bullied girl tries to disappear so the eyes / will close and / the words will stop and / when at last the words do stop / daddy thinks s i l e n c e is golden / but bullied girl knows an abomination— the wire cut / the thread b r o k e n / and her third eye that normally praises / the ubiquity of trees / striated leaves making chlorophyll that keeps her alive / a sky conversing with the soft spirits / of her grandparents / *meyn tereste* / six years old / running from their countries / at the end of a burning stick / instead her third e y e / sees danger / is always running / past fire and bullet / *shayna punim* alert for the kid / running / *shayna madela* burning / who would declare her / dead you are dead / dead / dead.

You're supposed to be writing a love song to yourself

& all that comes to mind is the vision of a three-year-old girl with strawberry blond curls held back by a green headband, her slate blue eyes hold everything the universe can unravel. White socks uneven, shorts pulled up too high, she's clutching a rag doll that she held day after day until the doll was lost. Then she took the doll's name & when you hear her parents calling her by it, you can feel her smile, peach nectar on the tongue. Every part of her is holy, from bruised knee to dirty fingernail to the blush in her cheek. She is silk & scratch, skin & trust. She is God's perfume, which you inhale. You want to tell her you love her, but when you part your lips to speak, your throat closes. The only sound that emerges is sobbing. So, you open the desk drawer & pull out the photo of yourself at three years old, square with old-fashioned white border. You look to see if you've missed any detail. You set the photo on your desk. Maybe tomorrow you will love yourself enough.

Sometimes I Imagined a Knife

Sometimes I imagined my arm.
Always my left. I would take
my knife, clean and sharp, sweet
ivory-carved handle, and slice

precise one-and-a-half-inch pieces,
fingers to wrist, moving up my arm
to my shoulder. I'd survey
the burnished droplets,

slipped veins, ripped muscle—peace.
Then eyes sealed, lid upon lid,
eyelash upon eyelash each
skin cell a bouquet of nerve endings.

When I'd open my eyes, I'd see
my arm all of one piece, breathe
in the scent of a funeral, follow
the marbled casket of a nine-year-old

girl lowered to dirt. Glancing above
the sycamore tree, I see her
floating, white daisies in braided,
rust-boned hair. I know now,

she is me. Arms outstretched,
she offers her heart, her white lace

dress dripping spinning helichrysum.
When I take her heart, I notice

purple petals, green sepals, yellow
pistils, all growing from the palms
of our hands. When I look up,
she's gone. In her place, a rotted

trunk, putrid leaves and dried red roses,
brown at the edges. But that was then.
I have no need for the knife, anymore.
Alchemy has turned metal

into something malleable, soft.
Now, when I read about the deaths
of Ashlynn Connor, Rachel Ehmke,
Erin Gallagher, Felicia Garcia,

Tiffani Maxwell, Rehtaeh Parsons,
Audrie Pott, Phoebe Prince,
Marjorie Raymond, Amanda Todd,
in an illuminated breath, seconds

before the train crash, before the bus
brakes, before the red wrists,
before the hanged heads, I hand
each and every girl my knife.

The Crone Who Appears in My Dreams, or When Will We Stop Hurting Ourselves?

The X-ray reveals a spot on my thyroid.
The doctor's office is white, and the doctor has small hands.

At night I fall asleep to the *thunk thunk* of dusty-white moths
hurling themselves against the windowpane, gunning for the light.

In my dream, the doctor says, *You have a spot on your thyroid*,
hands me a prescription he has written, folded like an origami

crane, flying away. I gather my sweater, green with pearl buttons,
pull the crane from above our heads and put it in my pocket.

In the next room a nurse dressed in white scrubs and white
socks and white shoes, unfolds it. She has black hair

and skin like first frost. Her eyes are brown and unblinking.
I cannot turn away from her gaze, her breath fills the room

with air—she is the lungs of the room holding me
with her breath, *The doctor has ordered flagellation.*

I don't know why I don't question the diagnosis or the cure.
The nurse motions to the exam table, and I lay my head

on the pillow. I lay bone and sinew and muscle and heart
and limb—I lay the whole territory of myself down.

The nurse closes iron locks attached to chains around
my ankles and wrists, then reaches under the table,

pulls out a leather whip. As long as my body.
As thick as an arm. My stomach clenches. She raises

the whip in slow motion, and it snaps above me
like a night-horse arcing in fear at a crack of thunder.

I suck air. Every cell and follicle of my body is aware
of the whip. The skin on my leg tightens and just before

the whip reaches my thigh, I hear a howl, a sound
that smells like a lake of rotting leaves. The howl

becomes a word—no—and the word echoes through
the chamber. *I was wondering when you would finally*

say no. She is old. She helps me to my feet, her hand
at the small of my back. She walks me through

her private door, and I step into a forest with flowers
the size of melons and a gentle rain

like softness in the ear. The nurse-turned-crone
writes in her notepad. *Presents with spot on thyroid.*

Spot is dissolved. Weeks later I return to the doctor with small hands and a white office. He tells me

that in the newest X-ray, the spot has disappeared. *It must have been a shadow in the film.*

Medusa

Medusa shakes her rage her snake-
eyes & hair I'd love to touch my
curls hers touching this gaze my eyes
of disruption she was seduced you say
tell it to the mountain I say tell it
to the sky tell it to every man the sins
of every man come to vanquish her
name & step on her head they can't look
in her eyes that gaze they turn to stone
how we turn to stone every time a person
asks what was she wearing was that vodka
she was drinking who does she think she is
to turn so much beauty & not owned by a man?
Channa's sisters call her a liar they called my
beautiful friend a wicked liar to ruin the family
name but her father raped her & sisters
abandoned her on an island named Grief
with this gift to look into a stranger's eyes
& know their own rage will turn them to
stone no warning—how she'd love to have tea
add honey & friends & lemon a few cookies but
these truthful eyes what does it look like
Medusa who has seen the truth & lived with grit
while the world re-tells her story the salient
parts all wrong it's not your story at all what
has she seen what evil turned her heart turned
the blood on our lips the crush of our breath

we turn & turn to stone like Lot's wife
who wasn't even given her own name how
dare she turn for her daughters [& who is killing
or raping them] what vengeful god is this
not my god to punish a person for another's
actions what was she wearing again?
Sandra Bland should have been respectful
to the man standing on her head
demanding fealty commanding
what she's lost in this world is lost to us
Medusa was raped that's how it went down
& still it sounds like the result of her own
actions i.e. Medusa was walking down
the street & stopped for a coffee how about
Poseidon raped Medusa in her mother's home
her own sacred temple did you catch that?
Poseidon raped beauty beauty belongs
to the voyeur her mother casts her out
(how like Channa) men came to kill
to claim her rage for who likes a nasty
woman who would vote for a nasty
woman who cares what happens to a …
you can grab 'em by the pussy all day long
how I long for Medusa's snakes her skin
her arms & if I looked into her eyes I'd see
rain & roses faun & lemur sweet river
mists & skies azuring the night if I could

tell her one thing it'd be I am grateful
for my truth her stare my snakes her eyes
my hair her gloriously healing rage.

A Tale Not Told

Shahrayar is my husband & I will die tonight.
I am common, though beautiful & have done nothing
more than sleep in my skin & know myself as woman.

Father arranged our marriage. Beauty & modesty
would prevail, he said, for what man could murder
a fifteen-year-old girl? I would have liked to wed

father's chef. He creates delicacies from honey &
rose with flourishes of crème & flower petals.
He made certain my bowls were filled—pistachios

& pomegranates &— I would redden my lips
with cherries then admire the line of my breasts
in the glass. I am obedient & married the man

father told me to marry. Too many have perished.
I am haunted. They come to me in sleep & whisper
Shahrayar is my husband & I have died tonight.

Their eternity—no children, no laughter, no sunsets
or windstorms. No stars shimmering a darkening sky.
No lavender scented pillows. No red earth scent

after a rain. So many voices. *Shirin, Shiri, Shirin,
you will die tonight* like crickets on the warmest
eve, insistent, persistent, comforting. Women

murdered in their wedding beds. Split like a seam,
blood ribbons. They tell me I am not clever & neither
were they. I wish I were clever. I wish I knew

how to keep myself alive—what were their dreams?
Do you know me? I am an artist. My dainty wrists
good for something—father sells my watercolors,

puts his name on them. I paint trees. Sycamores
that sleep. Willows that weep. I would like to sell
my paintings & live on my own. I would like to live.

You see how foolish I am? Foolish, beautiful girl.
Shahrayar is my husband & I will die tonight. *Shiri,
Shirin, Shiri, you will die tonight.* Soon, we dead,

numerous & shimmerous souls, wisps of light—
fireflies in flight whispering in the next bride's ear,
Shahrayar is my husband & I will die tonight.

You Don't Have to Be Good

What I'm asking is when will they stop murdering little girls—decomposing bodies under scrub brush teddy bear yards, blood ropes necks twisted? I'm with my niece surrounded by spruce & black oak, a sky as blue as lapis, the patter of unseen deer & mice a soft trill through the forest. Kate has planted herself across the yellow line on a private road, the ascent too much for her defiant bones, arms crossed, five-year-old legs splayed, body secured to pavement. *I won't move unless you carry me.* Her father had promised to meet us but he hasn't shown so I try *whoever makes it to the top first wins* to no effect. Unable to lift or carry her, in my fear & desperation to keep her safe, imagining a car around the bend splattering the last bits of her across asphalt, I throw out the only card I have left—*I know you are such a good girl you'll get up right now and walk with me.* Why did I think that would work on my niece, all vinegar & obstinate blood, her determination a sport of Olympic proportions? When her response comes through lungs at full volume, steady & sure—*I. Am. Not. A. Good. Girl.*—face red, spittle around lips, I know the answer to my question. I can feel the souls of all the murdered girls converged & dancing their skinned knees purple tennis shoes red ribbons. I know this moment is transformational, that the soft chemistry of my DNA has been altered, that Kate is the unknown X the equation solved. The culmination of genetic strands reaching back to the beginning of time has given me permission to express the full texture of my being. I am certain there are others like her blooming all over the country; the season is now. I move down the road to the bend & breathe the scent of wild currant, alert to flag any vehicle, letting Kate decide when she's ready & when she's willing to head up the road.

The Sparrow

I emerge from my house, an ocean of breeze in every tree, sun at every corner, fledglings flocking the garden each the size of a thumb. Gray & tiny, one becomes disoriented as I walk past. I speak to her in a soft tone but she turns herself on her back desperate to right tiny talons & downy feathers. She jumps down stair after stair toward the garage until she lands at the bottom. I gentle my voice as she chirps to the other sparrows nesting in roof shingles. I leave hoping her mama will help when I am gone, but in a few hours when I return, she is still at the bottom step alone & I think *orphan like me* in the dark corner what will I do to carry God into these stairs? I knock on my neighbor's door, my neighbor who once drove twenty miles to bring two hummingbird chicks to sanctuary after their mother didn't return to nest. My neighbor coaxes the baby sparrow inside a box, her halo tender & kind while the mama flies above our heads to keep us away. We carry the box to the front garden of recently planted geraniums & purple sedum & blue dymondium grasses—beauty we've ordained to contain sorrow. We leave the sparrow chick to a flurry of feathers & chirrup & trill. She remains planted, but eventually (and this is when I finally let the breath out of my lungs) she flies away. A dozen sparrows fly to the trees above me—cacophony of chirp & breeze at the neck, branches dancing against blossom.

These days are hard

We are amulets of divination. We throw crenellated runes at dusk—they return as dust. We sit upon a wastrel's throne, throwing stones at midnight. Joy is scarab, is amethyst & we approach with the merriment of an axe. We toss coins into a fountain hoping for some slight change, anything to renew us, but we lack wisdom. Instead, we exalt the courage of scissors—only we forget precision &, yes, these days are hard, a cracked boot against the incessant dawn. We are small blue buttons on God's raiment attempting sorcery to build a palace & when it all goes to shit, we seethe & seep, & yet, there's gratitude for each sapphire in hand. Because who among us has not received a blessing at the end of a spear?

Two

A Map of Every Undoing

The air is warm this afternoon & there is no rain.
There is only the sound of what's missing, quiet & insistent—
tiny footfall, a lover in the next room
scratching out novels with his pencil.

That was the dream for so long, high ceilings,
art on the walls, a cathedral window overlooking
a copse of trees—apples falling to the ground.

And still the bread is in the oven, the soup
simmers atop the flame, a table setting for one.
The shaman said there is no room for—
my heart, the drum-
noise of violence expanding
my lungs each day. The scars live
in the skin, a map of every undoing.
There's a hole in my solar plexus
the size of a cannonball &
I'm bleeding out,
    but the soul knows how to heal.

        I write my escape,
         blood drying on page after page,
        folios of fire poppies—

Who am I to speak of beauty?
Who am I not to?

Witness

for my mother

Imagine her.
She is sitting at the kitchen table,
pink violets in the window boxes,
the dull bulb of stove.
She sobs so deeply
there is no sound
only her shifting bosom,
her head in her hands.

She sees you in the doorway,
tells you she now knows
leaving her mother alone
to move to a distant city
killed her.

Imagine you want to feed her
pomegranate seeds, only seven.
Name her Persephone in reverse
so she can join her mother
in the upperworld,
then return—
but you know there is nothing
you can do
but watch her weep.

Throwing Stones

I awoke from a dream,
    mother saying
        I don't want you;
she'd been turned to stone,
     a petroglyph inscribed with jewels,
her alphabet
           full with sorrow &

hers was a language
    I never learned
to decipher,
       but at what cost?

I took a hammer to the tablet
           of her
spent the day
       scavenging the ruby
bits & singing
    the detritus to a flaw-
          less sky.

My Sister is a Mermaid at the Bottom of the Pool

pretending she doesn't need to surface
her fins are swift & there's no shark she doesn't call friend

she ditched class with her best friend
he holds his breath longer than she can, not a merman—
just a kid who likes to dive & has a pool

he doesn't want anything of her tits
the curve of her hips down to her tail
he tells her she's a damn good mermaid
he doesn't really know one fish from another

                        I wasn't there
when my dad's colleague pinned her against
the wall, tried to touch her breasts

though I read something she wrote down,
left lying around,
      it might have been her diary

the colleague brings flowers to my ballet recital in Central Park
—kick-ass pink flowers with forget-me-nots—
a bouquet ample enough for a prima ballerina

none of the other girls
gets flowers so big & I'm embarrassed
he felt up my sister

it's quiet at the bottom of the pool, she writes
I can just be myself.

Triptych in A Minor

I.

I remember yellow
tulips in the blue glass

vase when Jodi's
father entered

her bedroom
his bony legs &

silver rings, the grip
on her ear

the blood
on her white carpet

as he dragged
her away

his bathrobe
hanging open

his penis
in full view

the screech of her
begging for mercy

forgive me father
her voice a chalkboard—

laced hieroglyphics
of contrition,

but no mercy
was shown that night

her skin red,
stinging, seven

birthday candles
lighting her face.

II.

My sister's face—
morning's glory

at the kitchen
table, golden hues

down her back,
she asked father

for cash
to buy a new bra

& he pulled
bills out of his wallet,

so I asked for money
to buy band-aids

& mother snorted
coffee out of her nose

'cause my breasts
were tiny—

I meant to be funny
but father said

don't ever demean
yourself again

I told no one
about "uncle," his hands

across my thighs
at the family picnic

or the boys in school
who rubbed my ass—

I swallowed it all
until I was starving.

III.

I starved my young body,
disappearing

female signifiers
beneath the rice-paper

lamp, its ochre light
across the keys

as I practiced a piano
sonata in C minor

ivory under my fingers—
I stopped playing

lost in reverie, wondering
why I was born a girl

when it was clear
that boys

had the advantage,
so I begged God

to make me happy
instead of smart

but I was wrong then,
the bargain was not

smart or happy, male
or female,

the bargain
was really a prayer—

show me O father
a simple sweetness,

grant me the dignity
of respect.

Sonnet for Icarus' Older Sister Who Would Have Invented the Aeroplane Had She Not Been Married Off for Gold. Also, She Can Divine the Future.

I fly with red-tailed hawks over fields of asphodels, a dream too soon
to wake from. Doomed to babies & brushing my hair. O sweet Icarus
boy who runs slowly, loves the pull of earth & his feet planted, collects
lavender & sage, mint to balance the body's humors, women's work
that would bring him shame—instead we'll pay for our father's sins.
Late at night, the house quiet, Icarus teaches me what he's learned.
How I love him, his head of curls. I have studied well & these books—
poetry, geometry, though father must never know what I have learned.
Imagine landing in a meadow of orange scrub, navigating wind pressures
& fluctuations, kalos eidos shapes shifting in my mind, triangles, rhombi—
If I were allowed, I'd build a flying bird to save my brother. I can imitate
the lift of eagles & want to soar. Look at me! Brown hair, bold chin,
amber eyes. I am disappeared from history. Lachesis, Clotho, Atropos
must you cut his thread? This boy, terrified of heights, not an ingot of pride.

A Walk with Mist at Sunset

I fold myself on the line

& refold until my heart
shifts, releases forgiveness

like tea from kettle to cup.
It is this life I exhale

birthing the rush & cedar petals
against silk, against gray

cloud, then inhale what finds me.
O how we require slow change

repeating embroidered noise.
Moving boldly from indulgence

to thoughtfulness,
my breath a destination

that shivers a way through
& does not repeat. Faith,

a great friend to solitude.

Cutting Diamonds

The girl on the screen takes a hard-boiled egg
   from a paper bag a handful of carrots cracks

the egg peels the shell   bare takes a bite
   egg then carrot until Lunch is over

We see blue sky interfere sun pattern skin
   jacaranda leaves flitter the girl's shadow

against brick & tile We see tight jeans
   arms like reeds   She is still hungry hunger

cramps the walls of her flat stomach
   through algebra history where coccyx hits chair

After school she hurries to ballet where a murder
   of teenagers compliments her weight   loss

When you ask me what it feels like to be hungry
   I say self-hatred   When you say shame is feral

I lie down   with violation & pain
   locked in until   escaping   my world

corrodes & dims   through each
   day year passing year when I hear a song

about a woman   perfection   balancing
   rosy globes   baskets of fruit   ripe

& sweet   &   Chaela with her halo   leans in
   Angel   he's singing about you

No   there is only so much my life can hold,
   a teaspoon emptied holds more

my bag of skin   my quarry of years   bones
   like daggers when the glint fades   *Angel*

he is singing about you   I rub ruins
   from my eyes   unaware of rock or shine   while rain

falls without thought   without reason   &
   like a pattern hewing to the golden ratio

the spiral expanding   until one day
   I am lifted   not a story carved in stone   but alchemy

the goblet hewed by fire   heat &   chisel—
   only then   the wine pours   like light

You ask me what it feels like to be lifted   I say pure
   I say love   When you say love is service

I kneel   & offer my hand   Today while eating soba
    in chashu broth   Ximena asks *Why am I here?*

She doesn't see Citlalicue's   stars   ancient
    tossed across the universe   into her own brown eyes

It's my turn to lean in with halo &   shine
    every blink & pinch   praised holy.

On driving all night to find the shaman who will help me &

then I breathe, squalls of air in my lungs,
a $30 white t-shirt

wet with dew, I bought from a store with a blue
awning, down the street

from where I live by the ocean, I am far from there
now; the awning gray-blue

like any sky at dawn, & now it snows & snows,
a hand in the air

conjures a different scent, sweet like juniper & cold
like rosemary, but today

clouds clamp the trees in a silver wrap with no loose ends,
here in the mountains

where sweat evaporates from my neck, I've come to heal,
my mind is split—

there's the me & the child me who is screaming &
terror rides us both

into a numb frenzy, the shaman holds my head in her arms,
There now, I got you.

Sage burns. *Let it out,* she says, *terror must have its day,*
& by that she means

repressed terror, & by that she means for me to take up more
space than I ever have before

while coyotes wild against the stars, wet fur & fangs—we are all
howling together,

& now a clearing, a quiet so dark the black sky lays out the cosmos
as if I belonged

to something majestic, instead of twisted on the floor remembering
what I never wanted

to forget, the child by the door, it never should have happened,
when he stole her light.

The Sweet Balm of Dappled Roses

I.

The wind caressed my cheek as I looked across the valley below,

could smell the sweat
      off my back and the scent of forest—
sweet juniper & also decay,
      trees rising, a cycle.

II.

An old story, shame & ignominy.

      Death was a door I wanted to open.

I was Leda seeking help from a mystic,

      no deceitful swans to trick me,

here, in the ancient dirt of the mesa.

III.

She wore blue shorts, hiking boots, pink socks.
Her legs looked strong, had walked her own map of healing.
She pointed to tracks in the mud, stones

                laid out like glyphs

        showed me where I was &

              with a little more journey
where I would be.

IV.

There's always love, I'll give you that—a hand
on the heart, a reassuring word,
        but love is a dedication, not a gift,
         & somewhere the pattern interrupts.

V.

The mystic's cat followed us into the forest,
sat on a rock,
licked his paw.

VI.

How is it possible that we ever lose the wonder
of two gray rocks rubbed together,
soft, & softly?

VII.

The wild earth temples the sacred—
quaking aspen, limber pine, a woodland
blanket of quietude, peace.

VIII.

> *You will not die.*
> *You will heal.*
>
> *I will hold this vision until the day you are able to hold it for yourself.*

IX.

It was true.
I had once inhaled the sweet balm of dappled
roses, feral with fullness, &, now, hawks played wind currents,
rising into thin air.

X.

There was weight to this darkness,
something carried.

You Must Not Disappear

after Edvard Munch's "Young Girl on Shore," 1896, Lithograph

Sprigs of moss thrum beneath your soles, your breath full with sorrow.
Hooded yellow orioles whistle moon tides as you turn. Bees buzz

in honeyed hives. White oaks extend branches, shelter from the rain.
Rain falls to comfort you, plaiting patterns on the windowpane.

The wind hums grace notes as you lace the whales' song.
And when you smile, contented with your skin, the earth spins its axis—

the spider's web remains. Go home. If you understood beetle dung
and sugar cane, the answer in a meteor's arc, the pull of pale

echoes, if you could feel the shape of love in every leaf and misted
flower, every grain of sand content when you walk past—

if you could see yourself as I see you, standing in stillness
at the shore, the world offered at your feet, then you would understand

the ground beneath you is holy because you are there. Go home.

Before We Break

A young woman sits beside me on the couch,
jeans loose on her hips, brown socks.
We close our eyes, guided in meditation.

> A forest of clear-sap trees,
> upended twigs, thickets of wild huckleberry—
>
> a woman moves closer
> taking shape through fog-wrapped skin—
>
> her step, careful as a doe.
> As she moves toward me,
>
> I recognize her black hair, a flutter
> of white birds flying from her chest.

I ask if she would like to know
what I have seen with closed eyes,
curious if the birds hold meaning

or if they are, simply, mine.
She says she's been seeing a shaman
to heal end-stage breast cancer.

Chemo has failed. The shaman
has asked her to imagine the cancer
as white birds, then let them fly away.

//

I was invited to Heather's memorial today.
She is everywhere in my mind.
How does one walk through falling

leaves and still praise the soft green
of them? How will we reconcile
the grit of who we are now—

the twilight bush and rose-ravaged
tendril, with what we are becoming,
a carapace that breaks—

> a glory of white birds
> returned to sky.

Rare As Red Beryl

While drinking fresh-ground morning coffee—
gray sky, fan purring through muggy heat—

I think about 5th grade, sitting with #2 pencils
laid out on the desk in the back of the room,

how the kids would turn & sneer, their eyes wild—
& still despair comes to mind so many years later.

Miss Misty, the teacher with a blond updo & plaid
skirts, either never noticed or ignored the cruelty.

One child, a girl too tall for her age with dirty shoes,
wiry hair, & eyes like… [I cry remembering their good-

ness] one child in a class of thirty turned & put
her swan-feathered hand on mine & whispered,

I don't care what they say, I'll be your friend.

Scheherazade's Reflections on Her Wedding Night

    Shahrayar illumines the storyteller in me,
        the conjurer of flying monkeys, petty thieves,
djinns & fishermen, elegant wives wrapped

    in purple & red flowing silk, the sweet-slap apples
        & follow-the-stars sailors. I reach for wisdom,
piety & pomp, perfect turns of scandal & the grotesque.

    I am the clever, the dubious, the greedy in every word
        issuing from my mouth. Years sitting on my father's knee
memorizing every story ever told around the hearth,

    with a poet's mind, the gifts of rhyme & child-
        like surprise, I studied maps, kings, seas, sages—
any book my father left for me.

    Dwelling in my father's love with a mother's pulse
        beating in my heart, I quickly find the heart of a story,
add a flourish of gold & abracadabra—

    we are the alchemical, the lion tamer, the soothsayer,
        the sultan-whisperer, the ladies wearing pearls.
I summon a boy who loves auntie's tea, a princess

    with bells at her ankles, swirling, whirling dervishes
        sprint from my tongue this night, this cold mournful night.
My big-bosomed belly dancers charm snakes, men, & giraffes.

Where would a story fall without persimmons,
        pomegranates, flat breads with olives? My punctuation
is sapphires, emeralds, stars shining in a husband's eyes.

        I must see the good in him, calm his bruised heart,
            his murderous intentions. I must tell a story worth
its weight in silver. I am called, I know my skills—

        I may be the only person to stop a homicidal maniac
            & transform his heart, with story. When my plot twists
dwindle, I'll call on the spirits of one thousand dead

        brides and beg of them, *Tell me a tale to heal this king's*
            treacherous heart & you will save a thousand more.
& then I'll listen.

It began with a flower in bloom,

& I walked alone across the park, fixed
my glasses so I wouldn't miss the sharp
contour of tree and bush, wouldn't miss
the men in shadow. Then, I needed love
the way a dehydrated woman needs water—
cascading & poured generously so a few
drops might land on my tongue. But love
is an inside job & the fountain was dry
& sun was high, cumulus clouds spinning
away. I left the bed. I left the room,
I left terror where terror lives—
in a dark, unimaginative place— & the antidote?
I pull tenacity into my stride, walk out
of the house, across the park, my legs
carrying me where I need to land.
As a toddler, I wore a blue top with a whale
appliqué. Even then I loved whales.
Their largeness, their weight, an antithesis
to my tiny body and small voice.
I would be safe in the belly of a whale.
Isn't that a puzzlement? A poet
aware she cannot control what comes.
So, I left the bed, I left the house,
I walked alone across the park, fixed
my glasses so I wouldn't miss the sharp
contour of courage which I pull on like long
socks across my thighs, higher and higher

until my tongue is ready & I move
like a leopard that no one can catch.

Red

I waited for him,
led him to a shack
in the woods
where my sister gets it on
with the neighbor boys.
He didn't know I knew,
didn't know I saw him do it.

> *Mary was a little lamb*
> *her fleece was white as wolf,*

I planned all day,
marked trees with my scent,
rubbed leaves in my hair,
left a trail like in a fairy tale—
bread crumbs and liver treats.

> *and everywhere that Mary went*
> *her wolf was sure to follow.*

Bold, dominant, unchallenged,
he never thought to fear
a ten-year-old, red-headed,
freckled girl in a hoodie—

> *He followed her from school one day—*
> *it was against the law;*

in went my knife
as he crossed the threshold.
I slit him right
down the middle, extracted
his heart. I was careful
to wear gloves. I rubbed
grandmother's knife
with a turpentine rag,
then folded plastic wrap
around the blade and placed it
like a peanut butter sandwich
in my pink schoolbag.

> *He never knew her innocence*
> *would be his fatal flaw.*

I buried the heart
under a sycamore tree.

Weeks later, in a nest of leaves
at the base of the tree, I found
a litter of wolf pups
abandoned and hungry.
I begged my father
to let me keep one.

> *It made the children laugh and play,*
> *to see a wolf at school.*

He decided a wolf
would protect me from whatever
murdered that poor man,
the one with his heart cut out.

> *"Why does the wolf love Mary so?"*
> *the eager children cry.*

No one would have believed me
if I said that man threw her bruised,
ragdoll body across the room.
I watched him kill her. Helpless.

> *"Why, Mary loves her wolf,"*
> *her teachers did reply.*

A Girl Needs Her Mother

The truth is no one asked me to hide.
I jumped the thicket & piled rocks

until a wall of misshapen stones, chains
surrounded what was left

of my thorned throne.
I dreamed of hands,

scratched & rusted nail
so threw the lock's key

over the fence, crawled
into the dark, gritted my teeth,

drew blood. Who can blame me,
a mother is no light.

She hides behind silk—
blue triangles against cream,

a scarf too tight around the neck
her head tilting

toward the grave,
our ancestors piled in an unmarked grave—

her fear resonant. I wanted to play.
Instead, I mothered myself.

I smothered every joy, howled
every peace against a raucous wind.

I hate myself was the litany.
I'm not really here the amen.

Everything I did, I did with my
right hand while my left

held mother's tethered heart,
dripping. One match, one flame

is all it takes to scorch stone
for the rocks to fall—

so many useless hatreds.
Repeat after me. *I belong.*

All the Goodness of the World

I was walking down the street & a woman walking her tiny, tiny dog, turned to say *hello dear* & it wasn't the words but her smile— I fell into a hole the size of sweetness & as I fell someone handed me a cup of compassion though it tasted like lemon & honey & someone handed me joy though it looked like a pink wool hat & when at last I stopped falling, I was back on the street, though it felt as if my feet were standing on white sands in clear water & O the kindness of her eyes— we didn't hug because we were strangers, but I wanted to— her eyes said *it's okay dear*, yes, yes, her eyes said *there is goodness all the days of your life* [as if all the gray-haired grandmothers of the world stood around chanting *hello dear*] & her eyes brown though they looked like yellow daisies— life had handed me grief though it felt like mud & life had handed me sadness though it felt like thirst, but in two shakes of a second, here on the street with wild orchids blooming, my heart opened & orange-breasted sparrows followed me home— all because a woman with a tiny, tiny dog has in her pockets, secret treats for everyone [not a secret after all]—

Three

It's dark & the ghost

in the corner is silent
& sullen with her gun-
metal boots & diamond tats—
she's waiting for hesitation,
a shred in the fabric
of my own self-love &
when I crack like a chandelier
at the high "C" the pitch is exactly
the sound of
      you don't deserve love

the thing is, today, forty-nine
thoughts out of a hundred believed
her, but honey, the glory came shining
because fifty-one thoughts
rode in on a shivering star—
      but I am love

the seesaw sawed
& I'm already at this party
& damn girl it's too late to turn away
because the drinks are strong &
the music is sweet, so walk away,
because I'm good, & you've
got no place to sit anyway.

Rose Petals

Father is lowered six feet under,
his casket directly above mother's.
He'd had a midnight premonition
he was going to die, which he did three weeks
later. He'd asked us to unearth our mother,
so that he could be buried underneath her—
she needs to rest on me, not the other way around.
My sister and I sat with the funeral director
while he reminded us about Jewish law—
never disturb the bones of the dead,
besides, there's a layer of concrete above her,
in accordance with state law, and the jackhammer?—
it would be expensive, not to mention imprudent.
On the other side of the world father would be
below mother. *That's how it will have to be*, I say.
If we want to get downright metaphysical,
above and below are relics of linear perception.
We're a speck of dust in an unfathomable
universe, so can you really say which end is up?
I'm flinging red rose petals on the casket,
grabbing every last flower I can find.
I want my brother and sister to throw
a few too, but I can't get their attention.
They're talking to guests, shaking hands, hugging.
I need them to throw rose petals, in fact
it's killing me that they don't see
the magnificence of the gesture—

my parents watching from above,
each petal a rune for a magnitude of love
and grief—we haven't even finished mourning
our mother who died only four months ago.
I stand at the edge of the pit, careful
not to trip my heels or fall in myself.
The cemetery plot my parents paid for monthly
over twenty years is prime real
estate with a view of the mountains,
white clouds twirl everywhere, whirling
a breeze in this wicked heat.
I lift my arms to dry the dripping sweat
which leads me to gravity. Starlings fly
over the trees. I spot blue jays, and a wood-
pecker makes a ruckus somewhere higher,
while I'm stuck, like a fly on sticky paper,
to a spinning globe hurtling through space.
The casket is plain white pine.
By the sound of it, we were cheap,
but it really is the sweetest casket.
The word my artist friend uses, elegant.
I detect judgment in her comment,
as if she hadn't expected my family
to have an elevated aesthetic—
or maybe my thoughts discombobulated
with sorrow. I mean who cares what she thinks,
we'll all end up underground, some day.

Father made their wedding bands of white,
rose, and yellow gold—precious metals of the same
family. Mother's fit inside father's, perfectly.
I know what's elegant—a life well-lived
with a person you adore at your side.
Toward the end, mother wouldn't turn in
without a kiss from her husband, and father
would admire his tilting-toward-ninety wife,
hair matted from sleep, wearing a stained bathrobe—
Isn't she the most beautiful woman in the world?
I rip the blooms off a few roses; drop the petals
in my pockets, for later, when I'm alone.
I'll lay the petals down, light a candle,
praise my parents' sixty-three years
together, praise their eternities.
A prayer really. A prayer.

A Nest of Every Cry

after Chris Roberts-Antieau's painting "New Wings"

She's a crenellated leaf
                the way a girl gloves
the red of her hands   has prayed
fire   from her own chest
        from her eyes
    while the trees photo-
synthesize   an elm, an oak, a deciduous forest
    a green sparrow
skyward   trailing the final breath of hymn

The memory of a sword against her breast / a hand over
    her mouth blossoms like blood in a river   only a memory
        & still   her wrists blooming again
& still   she bandages the wind song of angels
        the fallen, the heavy-
featherbare bird wounded by buckshot
as a   thread cleaves lace to fabric
    she stitches wings to birds
birds to wings
            saving some mortal thing
making a nest of every cry & terror
healing the down on which they rest
    her voice   like seed
here now

Inside Every Story

I'm telling Paul about the devil look in my pacifist father's eyes
the moment he tells me he wishes he could go back in time &

shoot the motherfucker who hurt me, even if he ended up in jail
for the rest of his life. Paul tells me he never could understand

why Joe, the smartest kid in high school with aspirations for medicine,
became a police officer. Until, twenty years later, Joe tells him

about sitting in the hallway as a kid holding a shotgun, trying to work up
the nerve to shoot his father who's in his sister's bedroom, raping her.

I'm watching Paul at a quiet joint in Montgomery sipping whiskey,
sitting next to Joe drinking soda. The wooden bar is uneven & the stools

have no backs, but the air is warm & smooth music drifts through
the sound system. Paul is watching Joe in the hallway where the carpet

is shab green, the wallpaper peels & the sister's cries are muffled.
There's some kind of dusty moon leaking light across the back shed &

the mother is passed out, an empty bottle of vodka on the floor.
Joe is watching his father, night after night, same dark hallway, same

shotgun. There's no redemption in this story. In a few years the sister
kills herself & Joe continues to arrest people doing bad shit, hoping

one day the story ends with him standing up, opening the door.

The Opening of the Heart

after Donald Justice

Now comes the opening of the heart.
Here is the morning, wet with dew.
Here is the light rising against sky
your arms extended wide as you stand
facing Jerusalem. Now the geraniums turn
in their beds. The pink hollyhocks lean
toward your tilt & bees lift & patter
against blossom. You know them, their honey &
pollen, yellow dust creating your name on their wings.
It is the inhale & surrender. You have waited
all your life to remember your home, lifted,
to sit quietly in your own garden, humming.

You said you were empty, there was nothing
for you, anymore. You watched the radiant
stars & dreamed to return to dust & atom.
But this breath, reassuring your lungs—
your ancestors reach across time & ocean,
ask you to live with a passion they never could.
They take your hands in their hands, caress
your forehead & whisper, *You are a joy to behold.*
A lark lands on the tree, calls out.
The teardrop leaves are turning, photosynthesis
taking your old wounds—& now there's honey,
a sweetness in the tea, a drop on the tongue.

Sunday Morning

I was walking down an empty street
in the sunny part of town
where the whippoorwills sang
from high up in the palm trees, the crows
called out, black as some holy
night, no moon, no stars.
The yellow flowers turned
in their brightened beds of flame,
my head low as any earth-
bound thing, I
slipped on a broken sidewalk.

They were waiting on the corner
by the street sign. She wore her brown
felt hat, sunglasses, he with his cane &
bowtie, waving—
they were together
again, holding hands.

Look at this day, she said.
How can you be
sad? They were both
halos of iridescence, not from pigment
but from the cut of their misdeeds, scars
like prisms, reflecting light &

at last I understood. She reached

out. I touched my heart, kissed
my fingers, walked on, knowing
had I tried to take hold, they would rise
like dandelion seed.
Gone.

Anahata :: Un-struck

There's a hole in my back
between the wing bones

as wide as terror but slight
enough to miss if you don't know

what you're looking for—
the healer said my heart chakra leaks

light & the night flies through me—
still it feels good

when someone caresses
my back as if the breaking

never broke & night never fell
& kindness is all I've known.

I cracked two crystal tumblers
brimming with red-blood wine,

they split when I touched them,
each on different days—

I'm just a clumsy child
picking roses & limes

& I've forgotten wholeness—
the glory & the god &

now a grown woman
whose feathers don't fly,

wings clipped, third eye
with dark glasses.

But look up dear one,
the sky is soft

& any bird can launch
from the nearest tree.

I Stay with My Parents' Elder Friends Who Live On an Island in France (Île De Ré) & at Eighteen I Learn How Music Heals

At eventide the fog rolls in &
the house is quiet. I find Jean-Pierre

      when there is a problem

downstairs, alone, pulling the album
out of its sleeve. He places the needle

      he plays Beethoven's Ninth
      Symphony

at the edge & I ask if everything is okay—
he & Simone have had a fight

      beginning to end

& I had gone upstairs, stared out the window
at the lighthouse & the dusty blue ocean,

      sipping cognac

but now Jean-Pierre pours cognac into delicate
glasses. The warm fluid blossoms

      with sinew & spit, listening

through my body & we step outside,
sit on the dock, feet in the water—

      until it's over. We go
      to bed &

while the booming orchestra, the holy chorus
rises the spirit beneath endless stars &

      in the morning

the ocean christens us at our heels—
the next day we three sip espresso,

      all is well

after we toast day-old baguettes, layer
the bread with butter & strawberry jam.

Perseus Turns Seriphus to Stone (So He No Longer Feels the Weight of His Burden)

We drove up mountain roads
above the din and tenor of Los Angeles
to witness the Perseid meteor shower.

We were teenagers, planting ourselves
as rocks against juniper and snapdragons
alluvial washes, nestled with fir and pine.

We were rocks hewed by river
and flood. We quoted Nietzsche
and declared absolute truths,

sharing coffee from a dented thermos.
As darkness settled, I sat next to Tony
on a jagged boulder, white boy

with an afro, thin and kind, his skin
like eggshell. I wanted to kiss him
but didn't know it then.

I remember only his profile,
curls reflected against stripped tree bark,
when he said, *Alicia do you know*

you are beautiful? I wanted the sound of him
like savoring the last bit of rhubarb
that's got the sweet-to-sour ratio

just right, and you want to feel it
on your tongue for as long as you can.
It was more than his words—

a tenderness roiling through basalt
and lime—because for one whole night
in his quiet glow, I was beautiful.

Troopers found Tony's body
by the side of another mountain,
in North Carolina years later. He'd taken

his own life. I wish I'd told him
he was my only friend who could stare
at a painting for as long as I could.

No wish could turn that meteor
back on itself to land at our feet.
When you're seventeen,

you don't know that something
someone says will feel like love
forever—words inscribed

on a mountain, the scent of dew
and sage tearing across the sky
one generous syllable at a time.

I Wish You Were Here

after the painting by Alexandra Eldridge, mixed media

Listen. I hear a stream
and know the world is in my house
in my hand, the house
by the stream in my hand
in the heart of the beloved.

Open your door,
open the door in your eye
to the sky
the immense azure of your mind.

There is a woman
who is a faun
who is a snake.
She radiates dreams
near a rippling stream
where birds flutter halos in the bush
& hawks loop a lavender mist.
Brick by brick
shaped by a shaman
draped in milk-flower petals
& cardamom buds
she hums by the side of the stream.

Through the seams of her days,
she tosses coins like eggs,
the pink & green of holy plumage.

She tosses coins to the children who play in her light.
She tosses pomegranate seeds,
the pink liquid on my chin
down my neck, across my breasts
in my hand in my home
by the stream
held in the heart of my beloved.

    There is a room waiting for you.

Here is my hand & here is laughter & here is solace
& here is my house where I live by a tree.

The Artist Has a Powerful Hunger, or the Artist Feels as Though She Can Fly

When I got out of bed this morning
I thought only
about whether to have
Quinoa porridge
with raisins or blueberries
and how much butter
was too much.

As the porridge warmed
I went outside to look
at the sky.
When I looked up
I saw a cloud shaped
like a marshmallow &
I opened my mouth.

That's when it happened.
I swallowed a murder of crows
whole—
didn't even
need to burp.

Sunset in the California Desert

Lush & quiet
palms verdant, dappled

trunks & spikes of green
over oasis grass—

lizards remind me
of survival. Beyond

where the crows fly
the mountains emerge—

infinite grays & purples, the imagined
edges of my hips & arms

release their line.
I am no body.

I am everywhere.
I float with ecstatic stars,

am the ruined light of eternity.
There are already cisterns of gratitude

for such loveliness.
O symmetry, O holy breath

fill my bones' marrow,
this depth of longing.

I am alone.
I fold to knees,

caress the water—
there are always tears,

but who has not stood
at the edge of beauty &

launched a taproot seeking rain?
I have learned to locate

love inside of myself, & still
I am sky, everywhere lonely.

I imagine a warm breath on the upper
lip, the sibilant "s" in my ear—

the intimacies of mountains
shift to shadow. The dusk

rays of sun throw ochre dust
across sand.

Find me here, O loved one,
this my prayer.

After An Exhaustive Study of the Girdle of Venus

1. The whiskey all sour went down sweet
2. on the tongue, his lips across my thighs
3. I name Eden, garden of bridge & gospel
4. & esteem for my parts—breasts, skin &
5. spit & the way he grazes, savoring groan
6. & delight, kindling the palms of his hands
7. I follow, eyes closed & the warmth of fire
8. as we coalesce, two oceans against tide.
9. I praise this love. I think heaven but propose
10. sex & revelry, ten enraptured fingers
11. across his brawny back. I bless my hands,
12. the lines across my palms & the absent Girdle—
13. my Venus birthing meadow & thorny brush
14. heeding the urgency of bramble.

The Girdle of Venus is a line on the palm of a hand, the presence of which was, at one time, interpreted to indicate licentiousness & debauchery in women.

Hay Truck

I got kicked off the hay truck smack in the middle of nowhere, about noon. By two p.m. and I done know it was two p.m. on account of the watch Billy give me the day I had to leave so as I could keep time on account of my being late for just about everything. Anyway, by two p.m. I was a fit full of lost so I sat down on a boulder set up against a tree and leaned on my knapsack, looked up past the long twisty branches reaching for the sky. That sky laid out bluer than my mama's eyes. I pulled an apple out of my bag and took a bite or two, got lost again in my own thoughts, remembering mama's tears. I don't know what happened then, maybe it was the cool breeze or the slant of the sun or the memory of my mama's love, but my body hummed some kind of wonderful, and I knew peace for the first time. Seventeen years of life and the first feeling of peace. Peace. As if the world stepped out to greet me and God kissed me on the forehead and told me everything was gonna be all right. Imagine that, all on account of getting thrown off the hay truck on account of being a girl, which they never would have known if I hadn't a bled through my jeans.

We've Both Lost Patience for Men with Indigo Hands

If you come home from high school and find your mother in the kitchen, breaking a dinner plate across the sink.

If your mother tells you that when she was at work, a business she built, a client reached over and patted her head.

If this man told your mother she was so cute and how about a discount, honey.

If you stand on the chair, for emphasis, and tell your mother she has more intelligence in her pinky finger than this man in his whole body.

If you wave your pinky in the air for the count of one-one-million, two-one-million, three-one-million… to make your point.

If the next day when you come home from ballet rehearsal your mother tells you the man came back and she waved her pinky at him, repeating what you'd said.

If the man apologized.

If your mother kisses you—*thank you, daughter.*

If your mother is off-the-charts brilliant.

If your mother sacrificed finishing college to put her brother through grad school.

If your mother says to you one night with tears in her eyes, *I wonder whom I might have been if I had gone to Harvard.*

If you know she means her brother invented things, and she was smarter.

If you get angry when you think of this because it's still so hard to be a woman in business, hard to be a woman at all.

If you too wonder whom she might have been.

If you think of paper pushers with their ink stamps and leaky pens.

If you imagine men with indigo hands.

If you discover indigo is the color of soul.

If you are grateful for even this brief intimacy between you and your mother.

If feeling grateful is the only way you will survive her loss.

Grandmothers, what I want to know

is how will my body rejoice
    in its own beauty
when there is no end
    to what shutters & cleaves?

I am spinning in your eternity
    your hands open, eyes closed
for God—but always toning
    & atoning. Each day

after my mother shed
    her body, she flew above—
a yellow butterfly lifting
    the early morning &

I walked among the cypress—
    this body not a prison
but a home, a root-bearing
    blossom. What have I left

to do but love every tendon
    & synapse that planted me
here? Grandmothers, I bless the tilt
    of your hips, your wombs,

your thighs, & this life,
    our hands circling candle

& flame, our faces lit with honey—
   is this how I learn to pray?

Galaxies

Is the woman
walking in the woods
finding firewood
or celebrating trees?

Is the man
selling oranges
remembering her touch
or grateful for symmetry?

The child laughing
in her father's arms—
is she imitating those around her
or has she glimpsed
the edge of love?

I want to give you
the slivered stars
in the sky—are they real?
Is the light an illusion
of separation?

How we center and focus
the details of our lives
as if collecting bits
makes us mighty.

We crave our dark
coffee with two teaspoons
of sugar, not three,
clinking the spoon against
the cup so not even one drop
is lost, and all the while,
we are stardust.

You want to count petals.
I want to speak of infinity.

She runs to the edge of time in pink stilettos.

A persistent waxing gibbous moon hisses across the sky.

Hungry rivers mist *colla parte* at her lips.

Shall I write your obit while drinking black coffee with cream or red tea with honey?

Which high-backed chair is closest to the horizon?

Your lazy profiterole sits on the plate, smiling.

We've both lost patience for men with indigo hands.

The city sleeps even though the bridge is luminous with illusions.

My girdle shines sadness through its hands like a sweet pea on the vine.

Pass the persimmons, you said in June, winking like a semaphore.

I opened her jewelry box and heard the sound of a cricket, slowed to a psalm.

Acknowledgments

There are many whose love and support ushered this book into being. Brandon Reim for the many hours poring over line by line as I began to write, playing with language and laughing at it all. Jennifer Givhan taught me courage and unflinching tenacity. Jenn named me poet, and with her support, I lived into that name. Rachel Kann, my first poetry teacher, who reflected the promise she saw. Gavin Frye who even when I forgot or got lost, carried with me the vision for a beautiful life. Lissa Kiernan and all the lovely teachers at The Poetry Barn who shared with me the magic of writing. Mariano Zaro who offered me my first reading, and then second reading, too. Elline Lipkin who honored me with my very first Pushcart nomination which demonstrated what was possible. Elline also taught me to be curious and daring in a poem. Alexandra Eldridge for sharing her creative life and allowing her art for the cover. The wonderful publishing team at Stillhouse Press, with a special note of gratitude for my editor Tommy Sheffield whose belief in my writing carried me, whose attention to language and meaning soothed me. My mother (in memory) who told me she especially liked when I wrote the hard stuff. My father (in memory) who lifted me and loved me true.

With immense gratitude for the editors, readers, and staff at the following publications in which some of the poems in this book appeared in some iteration along the way.

Altadena Poetry Review
    Galaxies
    She runs to the edge of time in pink stilettos
    All the Goodness of the World

Anti-Heroin Chic
    A Girl Needs Her Mother

Arsenic Lobster
    She runs to the edge of time in pink stilettos

Beautiful Cadaver Project
    In Praise of a Broken Sidewalk
Califragile
    Inside Every Story
    Grandmother Says "If I Were Twenty, I'd Burn My Fucking Bra"
Corvid Queen (Sword & Kettle Press)
    Scheherazade's Reflections on Her Wedding Night
Cultural Daily
    Triptych in a Minor Key
Fickle Muses
    Gretel
Gingerbread House
    Sonnet for Icarus' Older Sister Who Would Have Invented the Aeroplane Had She Not Been Married Off for Gold. Also She Can Divine the Future
    A Tale Not Told
Glint Literary Journal
    Hay Truck
Gone Lawn
    You Don't Have to Be Good, The Sparrow
The Hunger Journal
    Inside Every Story
    Grandmother Says "If I Were Twenty, I'd Burn My Fucking Bra"
InterLitQ
    Sunset in the California Desert
Ishaan Literary Review
    Daisies
Jet Fuel Review
    the solar plexus chakra is associated,
Journal Nine
    Medusa

Menacing Hedge
    Red, You Must Not Disappear

Minyan Magazine
    I am fashioned from a gourd

The Poetry Distillery
    Perseus Turns Seriphus to Stone (So He No Longer Feels the Weight of His Burden)

Rat's Ass Review
    It began with a flower in bloom,

Red Paint Hill's Mother Is a Verb *Anthology*
    Witness

Red Paint Hill Journal
    We've both lost patience for men with indigo hands

Rogue Agent
    Before We Break

Rose Red Review
    Sometimes I Would Imagine a Knife, The Artist Has a Powerful Hunger

Stirring A Literary Collection
    The Crone Who Appears in My Dreams

Tinderbox Poetry Journal
    Cutting Diamonds

Vox Viola
    Sonnet For The Man Who Invaded My Childhood or Only Alchemy Can Redeem A Life
    Anahata Un-Struck
    my sister is a mermaid at the bottom of the pool

Notes

"Wherever You Go / Notes from My New Mexico Journal":
"...rankest compound of villainous smell that ever offended nostril..." appears in Shakespeare, William. *The Merry Wives of Windsor*. Ed. William Aldis Wright. Doubleday & Company, 1936. Print.

"Bullied Girl"
The words *Meyn tereste* are Yiddish, and they mean "my dearest." *Shana punim* means "pretty face." *Shayna madela* means "pretty girl."

"Galaxies" was nominated for a 2017 Pushcart.

"Inside Every Story" was nominated for a 2017 Best of the Net

"A Tale Not Told" was nominated for a 2020 Best of the Net

"For The Man Who Invaded My Childhood or Only Alchemy Can Redeem a Life" was nominated for a 2020 Pushcart.

Alicia Elkort is a poet, writer, and Life Coach. Her poems have been nominated thrice for the Pushcart, twice for Best of the Net and once for the Orisons Anthology, and her work has appeared in numerous journals and anthologies. She was born under the New Mexican sky and has returned to live amongst the juniper and pine where each day she is renewed by the still-life of blue and cloud. For more info or to watch her two video poems: http://aliciaelkort.mystrikingly.com/

This book would not have been possible
without the hard work of our staff.

We would like to acknowledge:

TOMMY SHEFFIELD	Managing Editor
ALEX HORN	Director, Publicity & Marketing
LINDA HALL	Operations Manager
SCOTT BERG	Publisher
GREGG WILHELM	Editorial Advisor, MFA Director, GMU

www.ingramcontent.com/pod-product-compliance
Lightning Source LLC
Chambersburg PA
CBHW050327120526
44592CB00014B/2085